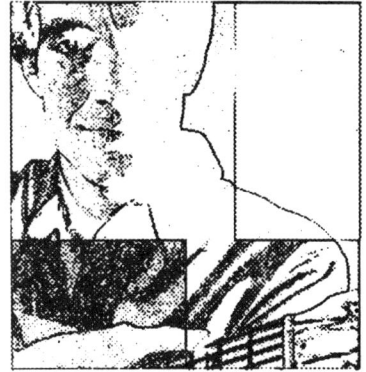

Chris Proctor

Ordering Chris's recordings, publications, and video

To order Chris's recordings, books and videos online with a secure credit card transaction, please go to **www.acousticmusicresource.com**, or call them at **(800) 649-4745**. For more information about Chris, you can check out **www.chrisproctor.com**. For audio clips of *Only Now*, you can access **www.rounder.com** and select Chris from their artist list. For other questions, please e-mail Chris at **Proctorgtr@aol.com**.

1. To order Chris's recordings, books or videos directly from Chris, select the items you want by checking the boxes below.

Recordings—
- ❏ *Under the Influence* (2000), Sugarhouse Records 007 CD, $15
- ❏ *Only Now* (1997), Flying Fish 665 CD, $15
- ❏ *Travelogue* (1994), Flying Fish 633 CD, $15
- ❏ *Steel String Stories* (1991), Flying Fish 554 CD, $15
- ❏ *Journey Home* (1988), Flying Fish 471 CD, $15
- ❏ *Delicate Dance/Runoff,* Flying Fish 357 CD, $15 (Double length CD of Chris's first two releases from 1983 and 1985)

Books and video—
- ❏ *Only Now* (with CD), Mel Bay 96903 Book/CD package, $20
- ❏ *Travelogue,* Mel Bay 95494 Book, $15
- ❏ *Fingerstyle Magic,* Mel Bay 95401 Book, $15
- ❏ *Runoff,* Kicking Mule 175 Book, $10
- ❏ *Contemporary Fingerstyle Workshop,* Homespun Video (VHS) $30 (This 80-minute in-depth teaching video features four of Chris's most popular songs broken down and explained. Hands-on instruction for all intermediate to advanced players regarding right-hand exercises for more independence of bass and melody, altered tunings, how-to introduction to amplification, partial capos, e-bow, practice tips, and much more.)

2. Total the prices and add appropriate shipping costs:
- ❏ Shipping to one address in the United States: $3
- ❏ Shipping to one address in Canada or Mexico: $5
- ❏ Shipping to one address overseas: $10

3. Tell us who you are and where to ship your order.

Name:
_____

Address:
_____

_____

City/State/Zip:
_____

E-mail address:_____

4. Send this form along with a check or money order, drawn only on U.S. banks please, to:
Chris Proctor
PO Box 520301
Salt Lake City, UT, 84152-0301

Please note: All foreign payment must be made in checks or money orders payable on U.S. banks or the U.S. postal service. Allow 3 to 4 weeks for delivery.

5. Questions??? Send e-mail questions to Chris at Proctorgtr@aol.com.

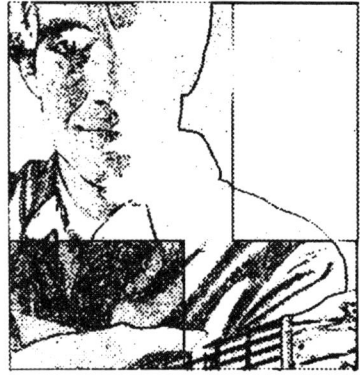

Chris Proctor

Ordering Chris's recordings, publications, and video

To order Chris's recordings, books and videos online with a secure credit card transaction, please go to **www.acousticmusicresource.com,** or call them at **(800) 649-4745.** For more information about Chris, you can check out **www.chrisproctor.com.** For audio clips of *Only Now,* you can access **www.rounder.com** and select Chris from their artist list. For other questions, please e-mail Chris at **Proctorgtr@aol.com.**

1. To order Chris's recordings, books or videos directly from Chris, select the items you want by checking the boxes below.

Recordings—
- ❑ *Under the Influence* (2000), Sugarhouse Records 007 CD, $15
- ❑ *Only Now* (1997), Flying Fish 665 CD, $15
- ❑ *Travelogue* (1994), Flying Fish 633 CD, $15
- ❑ *Steel String Stories* (1991), Flying Fish 554 CD, $15
- ❑ *Journey Home* (1988), Flying Fish 471 CD, $15
- ❑ *Delicate Dance/Runoff,* Flying Fish 357 CD, $15 (Double length CD of Chris's first two releases from 1983 and 1985)

Books and video—
- ❑ *Only Now* (with CD), Mel Bay 96903 Book/CD package, $20
- ❑ *Travelogue,* Mel Bay 95494 Book, $15
- ❑ *Fingerstyle Magic,* Mel Bay 95401 Book, $15
- ❑ *Runoff,* Kicking Mule 175 Book, $10
- ❑ *Contemporary Fingerstyle Workshop,* Homespun Video (VHS) $30 (This 80-minute in-depth teaching video features four of Chris's most popular songs broken down and explained. Hands-on instruction for all intermediate to advanced players regarding right-hand exercises for more independence of bass and melody, altered tunings, how-to introduction to amplification, partial capos, e-bow, practice tips, and much more.)

2. Total the prices and add appropriate shipping costs:
- ❑ Shipping to one address in the United States: $3
- ❑ Shipping to one address in Canada or Mexico: $5
- ❑ Shipping to one address overseas: $10

3. Tell us who you are and where to ship your order.

Name:

Address:

City/State/Zip:

E-mail address:

4. Send this form along with a check or money order, drawn only on U.S. banks please, to:
Chris Proctor
PO Box 520301
Salt Lake City, UT, 84152-0301

Please note: All foreign payment must be made in checks or money orders payable on U.S. banks or the U.S. postal service. Allow 3 to 4 weeks for delivery.

5. Questions??? Send e-mail questions to Chris at Proctorgtr@aol.com.

Introductory Fingerstyle Patterns

By Chris Proctor

Take plenty of time with each of these, and make absolutely sure that you are comfortable with the continuous thumb patterns of the right hand which is the basis for the style. In the first section, play these patterns in every first position chord form. They are written in C for your convenience. With your right hand, play the 6th, 5th, & 4th strings with your thumb, the 3rd string with your index finger, the 2nd string with your middle finger, and the 1st string with your ring finger.

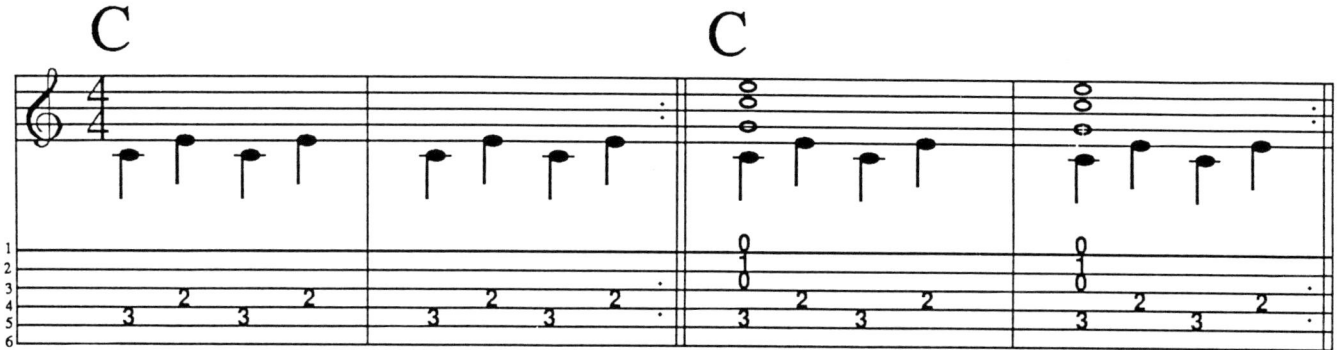

In this next section, always play a root note on the first and third beats in the bass. It should fall on the 5th and 4th strings.

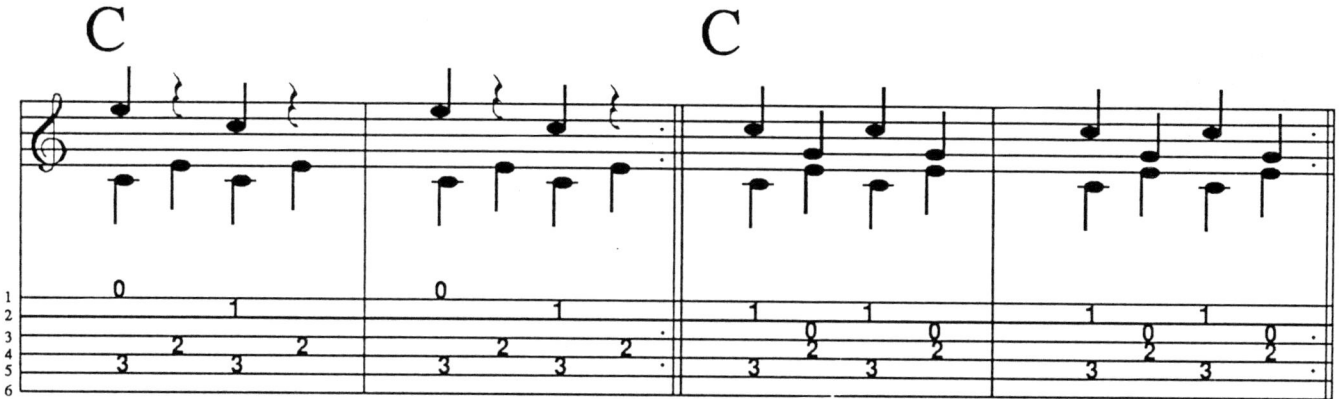

In the last section, the bass notes continue and the melody begins on the off-beat.

3/4 or 6/8 accompaniment pattern
Standard tuning

Key of D
Drop D tuning

Use your thumb to play the note in parentheses. Play it only if it doesn't interfere with the melody.

A FEW RESOURCES FOR FURTHER EXPLORATION

ACOUSTIC GUITAR magazine (415)485-6946, and *FINGERSTYLE GUITAR* magazine (800)664-8482, are the two bibles of this genre. Their advertisers are an encyclopedia of products which will be of interest to fingerstylists, from equipment to books to teaching methods to videos to recordings, and *Fingerstyle Guitar* also includes a CD of the music from each issue along with the magazine, which is an invaluable learning tool. I strongly suggest that you start with these two publications if you wish to learn more of this genre.

Good publishers who carry strong fingerstyle inventories of books include Mel Bay, Hal Leonard, Music Sales, and Accent on Music, and all of these can be found at your local friendly music store. Don't be afraid to ask them to order items of interest to you.

Record companies who offer recordings of fingerstyle guitarists include Flying Fish, Rounder, Windham Hill, Takoma, Narada, Acoustic Music Resource and numerous self-produced one-artist labels. Your local superior record store should stock, or be willing to order, any of these, particularly if you can find the item you want in one of their data bases or catalogs.

Video instruction and performance by fingerstyle artists can be found on Homespun Tapes and Stefan Grossman's Guitar Workshop, again available in most music stores and in the above-mentioned magazines. Good luck with your musical explorations!

For more information about Chris Proctor's recordings, books, videos, concerts, clinics and music in general, you can write or go on-line:

Sugarhouse Music
PO Box 520301
Salt Lake City, UT 84152

www.chrisproctor.com
Proctorgtr@aol.com
www.taylorguitars.com

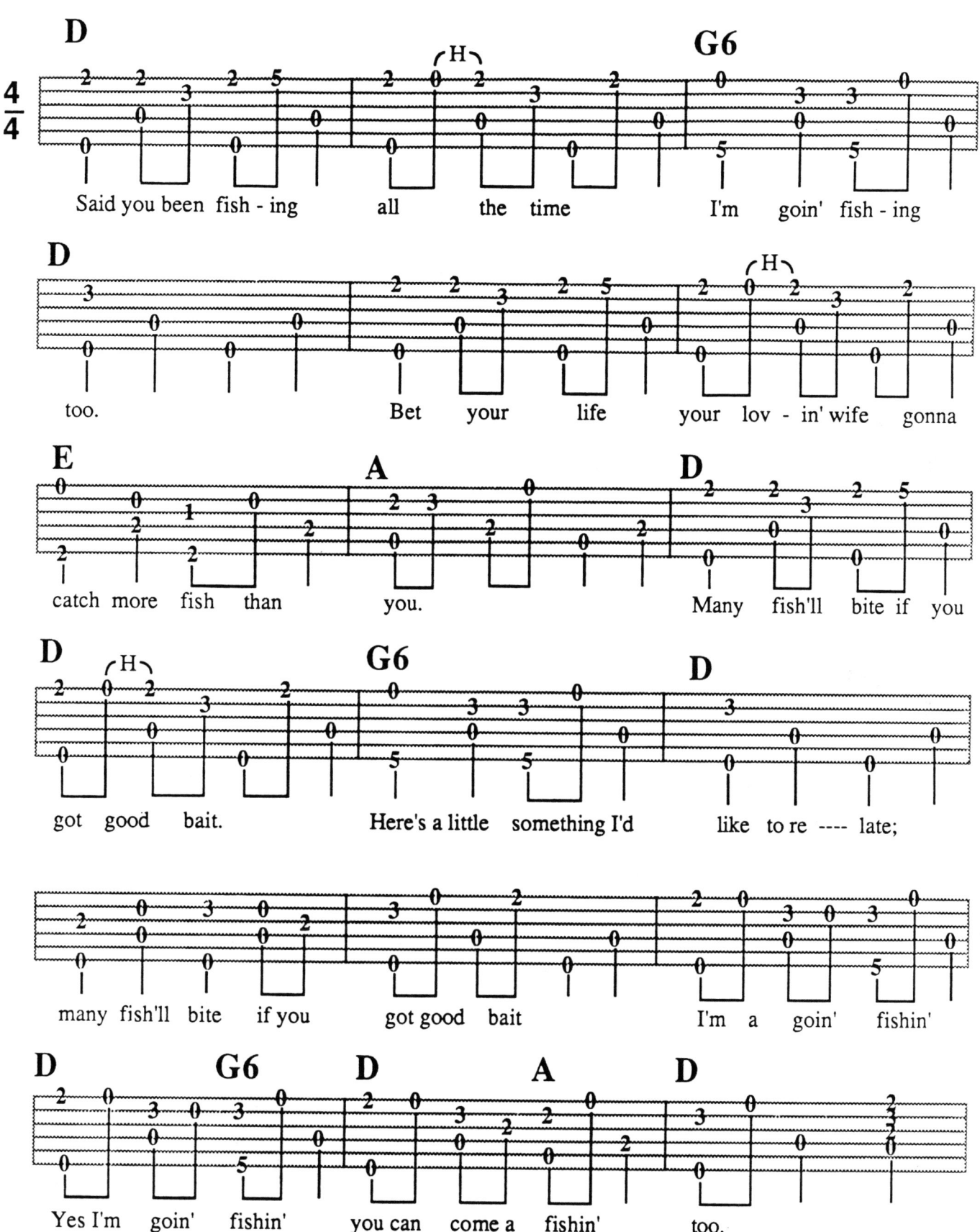

mel bay presents
CHRIS PROCTOR
only now

CD Contents

1. Adrenaline [4:07]
2. Tap Room [5:45]
3. Dialogues [5:45]
4. The Rambler/Kitty's Wedding/Langstrom's Pony [5:01]
5. Slickrock Lament [4:44]
6. Hotspot [4:47]
7. Only Now [5:08]
8. October's Window [5:28]
9. Anymore [4:52]

IN CONJUNCTION WITH ROUNDER RECORDS

© 1999 BY MEL BAY PUBLICATIONS, INC., PACIFIC, MO 63069.
ALL RIGHTS RESERVED. INTERNATIONAL COPYRIGHT SECURED. B.M.I. MADE AND PRINTED IN U.S.A.
No part of this publication may be reproduced in whole or in part, or stored in a retrieval system, or transmitted in any form or by any means, electronic, mechanical, photocopying, recording, or otherwise, without written permission of the publisher.

Visit us on the Web at http://www.melbay.com — E-mail us at email@melbay.com

Contents

Adrenaline 9

Tap Room 16

Dialogues 24

The Rambler/Kitty's Wedding/ Langstrom's Pony 30

Slickrock Lament 36

Hotspot 40

Only Now 50

October's Window 57

Anymore 64

Introduction

Only Now is Chris Proctor's sixth recording for Flying Fish Records (Rounder Records Group, One Camp Street, Cambridge MA, 02140). <u>Travelogue,</u> his fifth recording, is also available in folio from Mel Bay, as is <u>Fingerstyle Magic,</u> a compilation of selections from three earlier recordings.

Biography and Discography

Chris Proctor has been performing and recording his solo fingerstyle guitar compositions since 1980. He took first place at the U.S. National Fingerstyle Guitar Competition in Winfield, Kansas in 1982, and since that time has released seven recordings of primarily original compositions, mostly on the Flying Fish record label. He continues to tour, perform, write articles for the guitar press, record his music, and to teach guitar clinics for Taylor Guitars of El Cajon, California. He is also involved in GHS Strings in testing and design of their guitar strings, and with the Rane Corporation in testing and endorsing their acoustic guitar preamplifiers. He makes his home in Salt Lake City, Utah.

Recordings:

Runoff., 1983, Kicking Mule Records, available in cassette, or as part of
The Delicate Dance, 1985, Flying Fish Records, available in CD which combines it with the *Runoff* recording above, or as a separate cassette.
His Journey Home, 1988, Flying Fish Records, available in cassette or CD
The Windham Hill Guitar Sampler, 1988 Windham Hill Records, available in cassette and CD
Fingerstyle Magic, 1995, A compilation of favorites from three previous albums intended to accompany the book described below, CD only.
Steel String Stories, 1991, Flying Fish Records, available in cassette or CD
Travelogue, 1994, Available in cassette or CD
Only Now, 1997, available in CD only

Books:

<u>Runoff</u>- music and tablature from the above recording, (available directly from Chris Proctor)
<u>The Windham Hill Guitar Sampler</u>- Chris has one piece in this collection, *The Emperor's Choice*. Published by Hal Leonard
<u>Fingerstyle Guitar- New Dimensions and Explorations</u>- Chris has two pieces in this anthology. Published by Mel Bay
<u>Fingerstyle Magic</u>- Thirteen selected transcriptions in music and tablature from *The Delicate Dance*, *His Journey Home*, and *Steel String Stories*. Published by Mel Bay
<u>Travelogue</u>- the accompanying folio to the Flying Fish album, in music and tablature
<u>Only Now</u>- the book you hold in your hands

Video:

<u>A Contemporary Fingerstyle Guitar Workshop with Chris Proctor</u>- 1996 in-depth instructional and performance video for advanced beginners and beyond. Produced by Homespun Tapes
<u>Fingerstyle Guitar- New Dimensions and Explorations Vol. 2</u>- Several players, with Chris performing three pieces. Produced by Stefan Grossman's Guitar Workshop

All of these products may be found at your local superior music and/or record store, or may be ordered directly. For an order blank, please send a self-addressed stamped envelope to:

Sugarhouse Music
P.O. Box 520301
Salt Lake City, UT, 84152-0301

You can find Chris Proctor's products and his itinerary on the World Wide Web as well, at:
http://members.aol.com/proctorgtr

Player's Notes

As I reread my notes from some of my earlier books, I began to realize that some of the instructions are repetitive, and also that some techniques are hard to visualize when printed descriptions are all that you have to go by. This might be a slick pitch for my instructional video, but there really is no substitute for seeing this music being played, so I encourage you to do whatever you need to do to make this music, and this style come alive. Listen to the pieces, try to get out to see my performances and workshops, as well as those of other players, utilize videos when they are appropriate, pester the better players at your local music stores, chat on-line with other like-minded guitar heads, read the guitar magazines like *Acoustic Guitar* and *Fingerstyle Guitar*, and generally obsess to the extent that your life allows you to do so

Tapping- Players need to realize that tapping is no more than hammers and pulloffs that we've always used, carried to a higher order, in such ways that you need to think a little more like a piano player, with left hand-right hand independence. You'll find tons of tapping in *Tap Room*, not surprisingly, and quite a bit sneaking into *Hotspot*. In these tunes, much of the bass line is initiated with the left hand only, while the right is busy with harmonics, or other business. As in any practicing, please take it slowly. I tell my students that they should only practice as fast as they can play perfectly, and that to practice faster than that is to practice making mistakes, which is worse than no practice at all. A helpful image is that you are literally creating new wiring, new neural circuitry, when you practice- teaching your head and your hands some new ways of doing things. We all know that new construction is preferable to remodelling- that is, if we do it right the first time it turns out to be much easier than having to go back to remove our mistakes and restore the corrected process.

Slide- For complicated discussion of slide you'll need to find another resource from those mentioned above, but the basics are simple. Use the slide on your little finger so that you have three chording and string-muting fingers still in use, and choose a slide with a slight curvature to match that of your fingerboard. Glass is mellower and less sustained than brass, and in general heavier is better than lighter, provided that your left hand pinky can handle the weight.

Ebow™- The coolest gift to acoustic guitarists in ages is the gift of sustain, and of freedom from the characteristic guitar attack, and the Ebow™ provides both of these things. When you buy one you should listen to the accompanying cassette, which is very cool, but throw out the instructions, which are largely for electric players and which have little or no application for acoustic musicians. On some of my recordings I have Ebow™ melodies over normal bass lines, but on *Only Now* I use solo bowing, which is easier. Practice on the B string first, which is the easiest due to its low tension and high steel content. Later you might try holding the bow backwards in the palm of your hand and little finger, with the LED pointing towards the bridge, and trying to free up your thumb for bass lines. That is the beginning of a two-voiced Ebow™ style, but as I say, you won't have to do that in this collection.

Sweep Harmonics- By using your right-hand thumb to attack the strings, and either your right-hand little finger or first finger to lightly touch them at the same time, you should be able to generate not only individual artificial harmonics, but whole or partial strummed chords as well. This is one of the techniques which is easier to explain visually. You'll find this technique quite a lot in *Tap Room*, and in other pieces here and there. Those of you who play with nails only, and no picks, may have to experiment with down strums involving the right first finger and little finger to achieve the same effect.

Twelve-string octave strings only- On the song *War Games* from my *Travelogue* album I used this technique extensively, but it only shows up briefly in this collection, in *Slickrock Lament*. The right thumb needs to develop a more upright and lighter attack so that it can play the high-pitched octave string only. This technique, when used on the A, D, and G strings particularly, can summon high pitched melodies which are unavailable on six-string guitars, and which add to the range and harp-like quality of the tune. This is another technique which is better seen than described in print, but very worth acquiring. To my mind the twelve-string's big advantage over the six-string lies in those octave strings, and this technique allows you to liberate them and put them to good use.

Equipment talk

String gauges- I have experimented for years. For those of us who use lots of guitar tunings, light gauge strings often seem wimpy. Using DADGAD as my standard tuning, it seemed to me that beefing up the Two E strings and the B string made some sense, and GHS was kind enough to introduce a set of phosphor bronze strings called "True Medium," which have gauges of .056-.042-.032-.024-.017-.013 from bottom to top. For those of you who retune, they are well worth trying.

Guitars- At guitar clinics I sense the puzzlement and frustration of many players about such details as neck width, string action, playability, truss-rod adjustment, and so on. I strongly suggest that any serious fingerstylist should have a guitar which is in the smaller range of body sizes, (i.e.., not a dreadnaught) and which has a lower action, and a wider neck than is often called "standard." Keep in mind that this combination of features can only occur in a guitar which has the neck attached to the body at the exactly correct angle, and that few makers can really guarantee that their neck angles are correct and also correctable if the passage of time works some changes on your instrument. I prefer Taylor guitars, partly for those reasons.

Amplification- I have written lots of words on this subject. You amplification fanatics would be well-served to search the back issues of *Acoustic Guitar* for some of my articles on the subject. I will say this- if you are serious about your live sound, prepare yourself for an education in electronics, and for using more than one source in your instrument. I have found no one pickup which I can recommend on its own.

Picks versus nails- Another contentious topic. There is no one correct way to do things, as you can observe for yourself merely by taking a brief look at what today's state-of-the-art players are using. They are all over the map, from bare fingers to thumb picks only to chemically enhanced nails to Alaska pix. You need to consider your own musical preferences, your volume and dynamics, what the rest of your life asks of your hands and fingers, and make a decision based on those factors. You will need to ask questions and experiment before you find the comfortable solution.

Good Luck!

Adrenaline

This is an old-fashioned alternating bass speedster, and I have a lot of fun with it if I am warmed up. If not, I avoid it, for it demands a lot from both hands. The tuning is double-dropped D, which I have used for years but which doesn't seem to be that popular in the guitar world. You will want to mute the bass to your taste with the right wrist and thumb muscle once you get into the fast parts.

The melody has a lot of fast hammer-ons and pulloffs, and I suggest making those a separate object of practice. I would take the A section, bars 68-77, slow it down to a crawl, and work on it over and over. It is one of the central technical challenges of the piece, and contains big chunks of the hammers and pulloffs which are essential to successfully navigating this piece.

Almost all of my pieces have melodic variations throughout. If you see a repetition of an A section, for instance, you can assume that the repetition is not slavishly imitative, but rather has bits of improvisation, like a fiddle tune the second or third time around. In some pieces you will find long examples of this. My goal is to have you breathe your own life into these pieces, and the repeated portions are great places to do that.

In the B section, around bar 97, try using your left thumb on the fretted bass notes

Tap Room

Here's a fun, physical piece, which contains a lot of technical challenges. First and foremost, there is the tuning- EBEGAD, which you've probably not encountered before. Get acquainted with it first. What key are you going to be using? (Em), What chords do you need to learn to function in that key? (Em, A and Am, B7, F#half-dim.7) etc. Find them and learn them, or else you're flying blind.

Next there is the tapping. You will need to spend some time on the very beginning of the piece learning the rhythm of bass-slap harmonic-bass-ascending slap harmonic which is the crux of the music here. The right hand first finger is generally slapping two strings at a time and ascending as it proceeds, so that the first slap hits the A and D strings, the second slap hits D and G, and so on. Some times I substitute the sweep harmonics described in the introduction instead of the slaps.

This piece was designed to allow improvisation in the melody, but more improvisation and complex variation in the bass line as it moves along. The bass ascends, descends, tries diatonic, then more chromatic movement as the piece proceeds. The rhythmic variation is improvised as well, and if you hear me do this in concert you will realize that the rhythm of the bass is often shifting as well.

The third element which will challenge the player is the contrast between triplets in the bass and standard 4/4 time in the melody, or vice-versa. Bars 103, 119, and 143 are good examples, as is bar 175. Your right hand will need to learn this new skill, with fingers counting differently from thumb, and it would disappoint me if you were able to do this in a day or two

Dialogues

Here's a slower piece, a chance for the listener and the player to catch his or her breath. I intended this originally as a solo improvisational piece, but later changed my mind, changed its name to reflect its new duettish nature, and recorded it with mandolinist Matt Flinner. Either way I see it, and perform it as a call-and-response of sorts, a series of interactions between passages of improvised melodic statement followed by episodes of sustain and repose, where the beauty of the sound of the instrument and the notes and chords which have just been played are allowed to move outwards like ripples in a pond for a few seconds. Sustain is of the utmost, and the live, breathing quality which the classical players know as *rubato* is important throughout the piece. Try to imagine this as a dialogue even if there is only one of you- a dialogue between impulsive and restful parts of your nature, between the tempo of your days and that of your late evenings.

Technical challenges will surface during the C portion, around bar 94, when the A chord in first inversion will be hard for the left hand to play with the sort of sustain which this piece demands. In general, in fact, the challenge is the same- to milk the instrument's sustain and minimize the squeaks and chord position changes which detract from this sort of languid feeling.

The Rambler/Kitty's Wedding/ Langstrom's Pony

Here comes the Ebow™. Please refer to the introduction for more information and technical discussions of its use. After the intro most of the challenges are for the left hand. The right hand is going to mute the bass notes with the wrist and thumb muscle, keeping a steady dotted-quarter monotonic bass going for the most part until the third jig, when the thumb is suddenly called upon in bars 67 and 75 to play part of the lower section of the melody. For these notes your goal should be to integrate the thumb so that its notes don't stand out in the flow, and don't sound any different in their attack and quality than those notes played with the right-hand fingers.

The left hand has a workout all of the way through. High points are the fiddlistic grace notes and slurs which occur as often as I could get them in, the extensions of the little finger on the melody of bars 9-12, and the fast and difficulty melody which lies in the middle of the second jig, from bars 58-65. Take these parts slowly, and use them as finger-strengthening exercises if necessary, figuring that such exercises will not only solve the technical problems at hand, but also those other ones which require the same sort of finger strength or agility.

Note that the second jig is played in the key of D, rather than the G to which the guitar is tuned. It is not a big adjustment- your A chord is a simple bar across the second fret, and you have the advantage of two open D notes which helps free your left-hand fingers up for the strenuous melodic duty at hand.

Slickrock Lament

The twelve-string will require an attitude adjustment after a heavy dose of six-string, as will the slide technique after several songs of standard left-hand fretting. What kind of adjustments?

First- the guitar is tuned a whole step low, with very heavy strings. For ease of reading and for those of you who have an instrument tuned normally, I wrote the music out in the key of C, but I tune my twelve-string B♭FCFAC for this piece. I am looking for the most sonorous, low fat tones I can get here. The heavy strings and low tuning help in achieving those qualities. I use a heavy brass slide from the Latch Lake people, which gives me as much sustain and volume as possible, but it also makes control of the slide more difficult, and scraping slide noises more obvious, so it's time to polish the slide technique for those of you who haven't done that yet, to minimize the non-musical distractions and maximize the melodic potential.

The twelve-string offers us opportunity to utilize techniques not available on the six. During the A variations, I will sometimes play just the octave G string, which gives me a very high note above the capability of the other strings in normal melody playing. I referred to this technique in the introduction, and you will hear it here. Just straighten up your thumb and play lighter than normal, light enough to play the high note but not the low one. Also, during the B section, I am playing a chord on only the E, A, and G strings, because the rest of the strings under the slide are not tuned to that chord, and would sound horrible if they were accidentally played, or even if you got a little rambunctious with your slide and caused them to sound a little bit. The touch which you have to develop with both hands during that section, (Bars 18-21 and during the repeats), to avoid making the D, B and E strings sound, will take you a little time.

Hotspot

This may be the hardest piece in this collection, with the odd tuning, EBEGAD, and the complicating factors The bass notes are usually played between thumb and first finger, and that means that you will have to develop an independence between first finger bass notes and second and third finger melody notes which is somewhat unusual, and also learn to use the first finger in this dual role much of the time. Very exposed fourth fret harmonics in several places (see bar 41) in the piece will demand accuracy.

This is a composition of inner voices, and they must be audible. The A section almost constantly uses them, on the D string most often, (see bar 44 and beyond) and there are internal voices around bars 53-56 which must come out in performance of this piece, because they contrast with other altered voices during the repetition of that section at bars 114-117, in which one of those voices is kept constant despite the changing chords. The octaves at bar 150 are another very exposed section which will need work.

From time to time you will notice that some of the ascending bass notes had to be tapped rather than played with the right-hand thumb or fingers. This was of necessity, to keep the low bass pattern going, and it will likely make sense to you when you get to those parts in the piece. Good luck with this one.

Only Now

Here is another breather, as far as tempo, but not as far as the demands of the piece. In some ways these slow sustained pieces demand more than the fast ones. There is no way to cover for the missed note here, and small mistakes, losses of sustain, squeaks, ignorance of dynamics and of the correct feeling of the piece, are painfully obvious. I start out with melody only, to accentuate the exposed feeling which I wish this piece to have, and to magnify the importance of the harmony when it enters in bar 11.

The A section has many variations, both melodically and with the contrapuntal bass. Most of these are written out, but once again feel free to add a bit of yourself to these variations, and to make the piece your own. At the beginning of B there is a bit of a left-hand stretch, (bar 47) and again towards the end in bar 53.

The C section has some internal voicing which must be articulated clearly at bars 67-68, probably using first and third fingers of the right hand to play.

Some of the instructions from **Dialogues** also applies here- Play with feeling, let the piece breathe, like a singer would sing it. In fact, the name of this piece came from an incomplete set of words that seemed to present themselves during the composition process around bars 96-111, when I kept picturing someone singing "For only now will I" with the words trailing off after that point. Make it sing.

October's Window

Now we're in D tuning, one which you may have already used, or at least not an oddity like EBEGAD. At the risk of sounding like a broken record (a metaphor which is losing its meaning in the CD age) this song is built on the notion that you will be improvising the melodies whenever you repeat any of the sections.

I used Matt Flinner's fine mandolin playing and Michael Johnson contributed some sterling resophonic guitar, and as a consequence I laid back a little more to give them some room, but this, as all of this collection, is meant to be played solo, and there's no laying back for the soloist, as you well know. There may be places that you have a hard time hearing what the guitar is doing on the recording, and it's safe to assume that in those places you will need to step forward in solo performances as my sidemen did in the recording. There a plenty of variations where you do hear only or mainly the guitar, and those can be used as a basis for coming up with some of the melodic choices of your own.

The improvisations don't necessarily have the off-the top-of-your-head character of those of a great single note jazz improviser who is fluent in standard tuning. After all, we are trying to improvise in a tuning with which we may be only a little familiar, and at the same time as we are carrying on a solid bass line with its own ideas. Nonetheless, it is possible, and in this piece, very desirable to get outside of the basic melody and find ways to personalize this music.

During the D section repeat, there is an extra beat added at bar 66/74 which is not present in the first time through. Sorry, I thought that it added a little something

I used the oldest guitar I have- my original Koa Grand Concert from 1984. It seemed to suit the music and the key. I'm not sure if anyone but me can hear the difference, but just the same, it seemed to matter at the time. I also used it on the jigs.

Anymore

Since this is a vocal piece, you would expect the guitar part to lay back a little bit, and indeed, it does so, relying on relatively simple patterns during the accompaniment sections of the song. During the instrumental sections, the breaks and introductions, there is more to do. At bar 64 the hammer ons which ascend and introduce the break must be clean and loud. The same is true of the break at the end, when hammers at bar 143 and 144 are very exposed and important.

Other than those sections, keeping up a good tempo and staying out of the way of the vocal by keeping things simple are your only challenges. The B half-diminished chord might surprise you at bar 19, and the F/C chord at bar 49, but they are the only surprises.

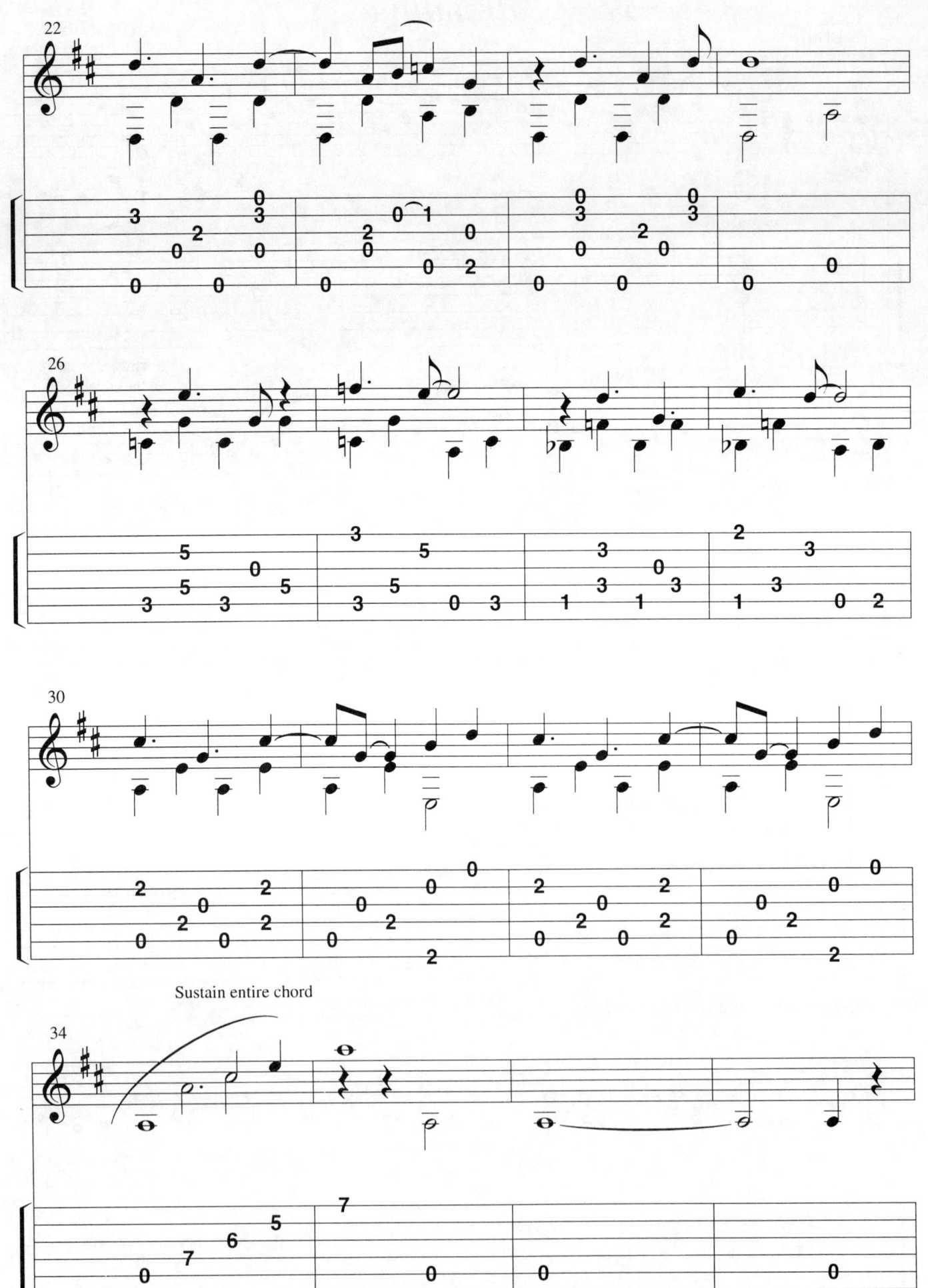

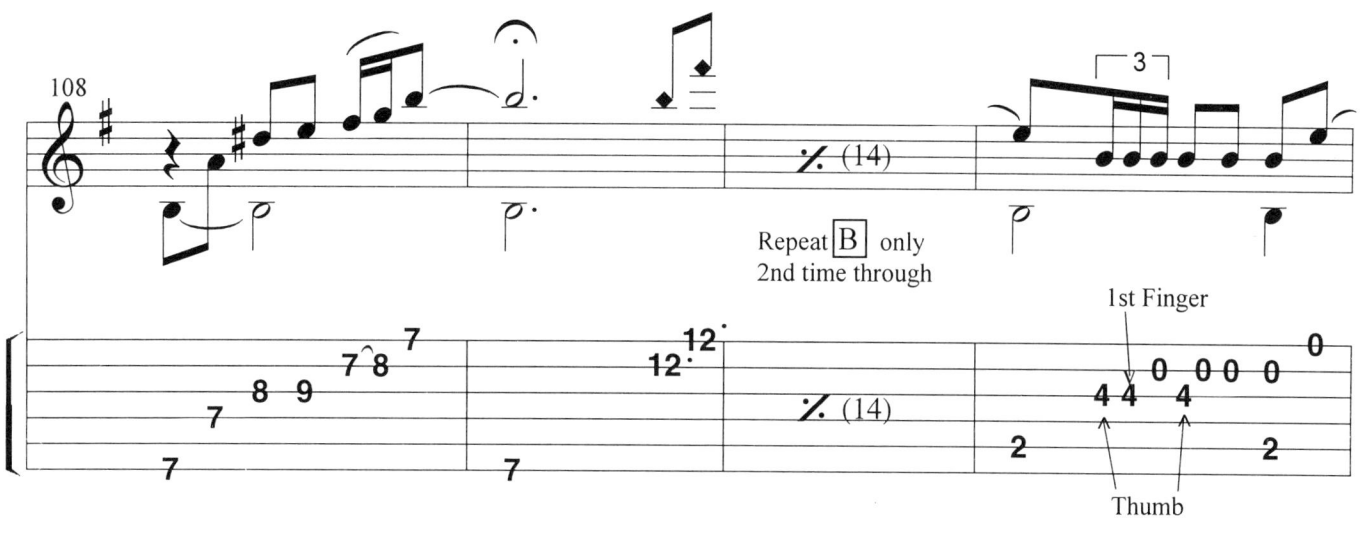
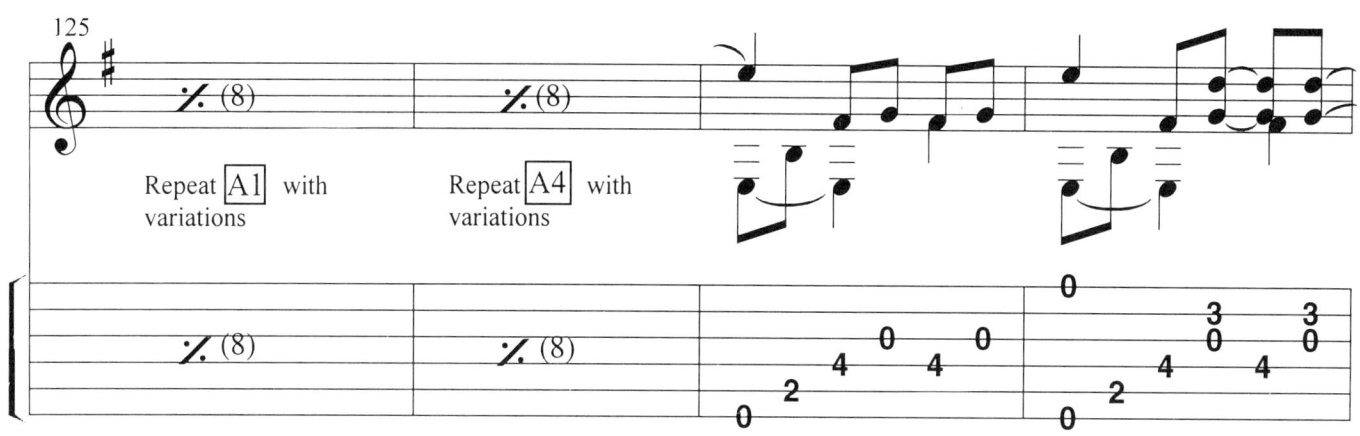

29

Langstrom's Pony

© 1997 Happy Valley Music & Sugarhouse Music. All Rights Reserved. Used by Permission.

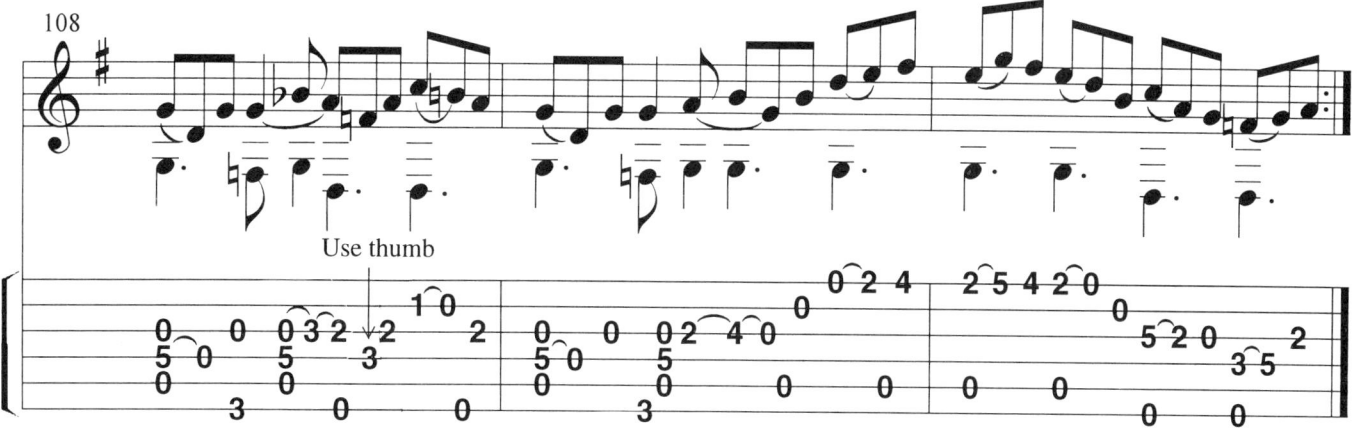

return to "The Rambler"

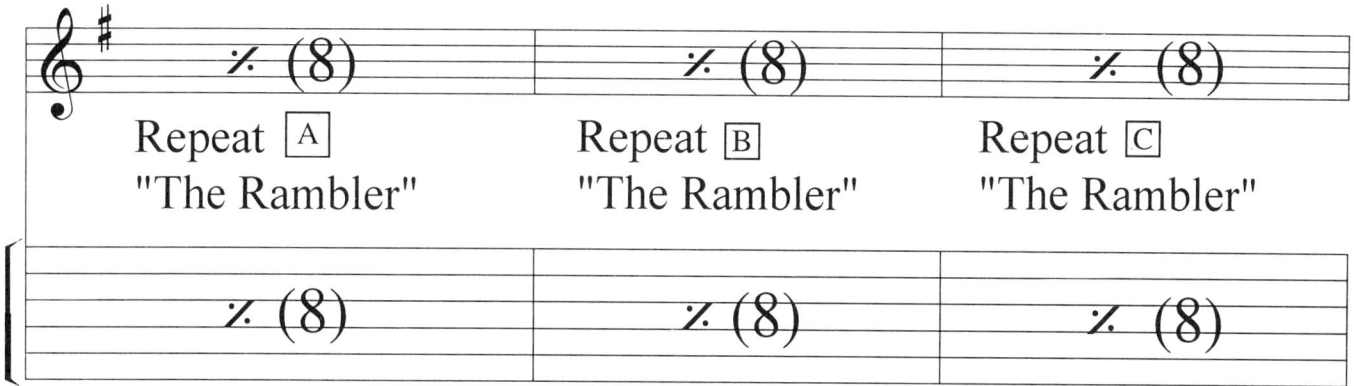

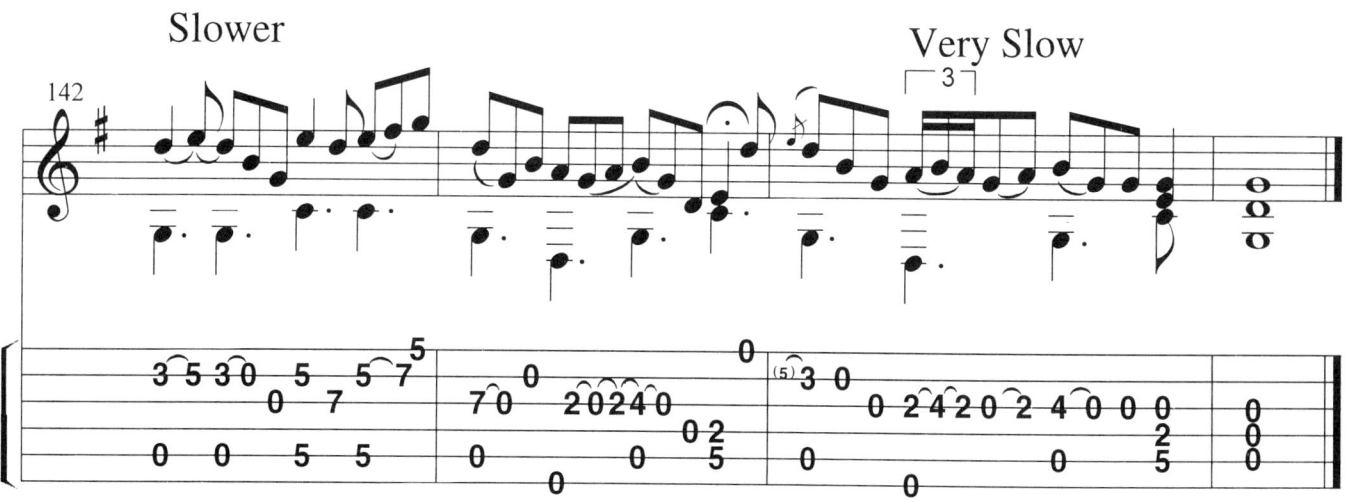

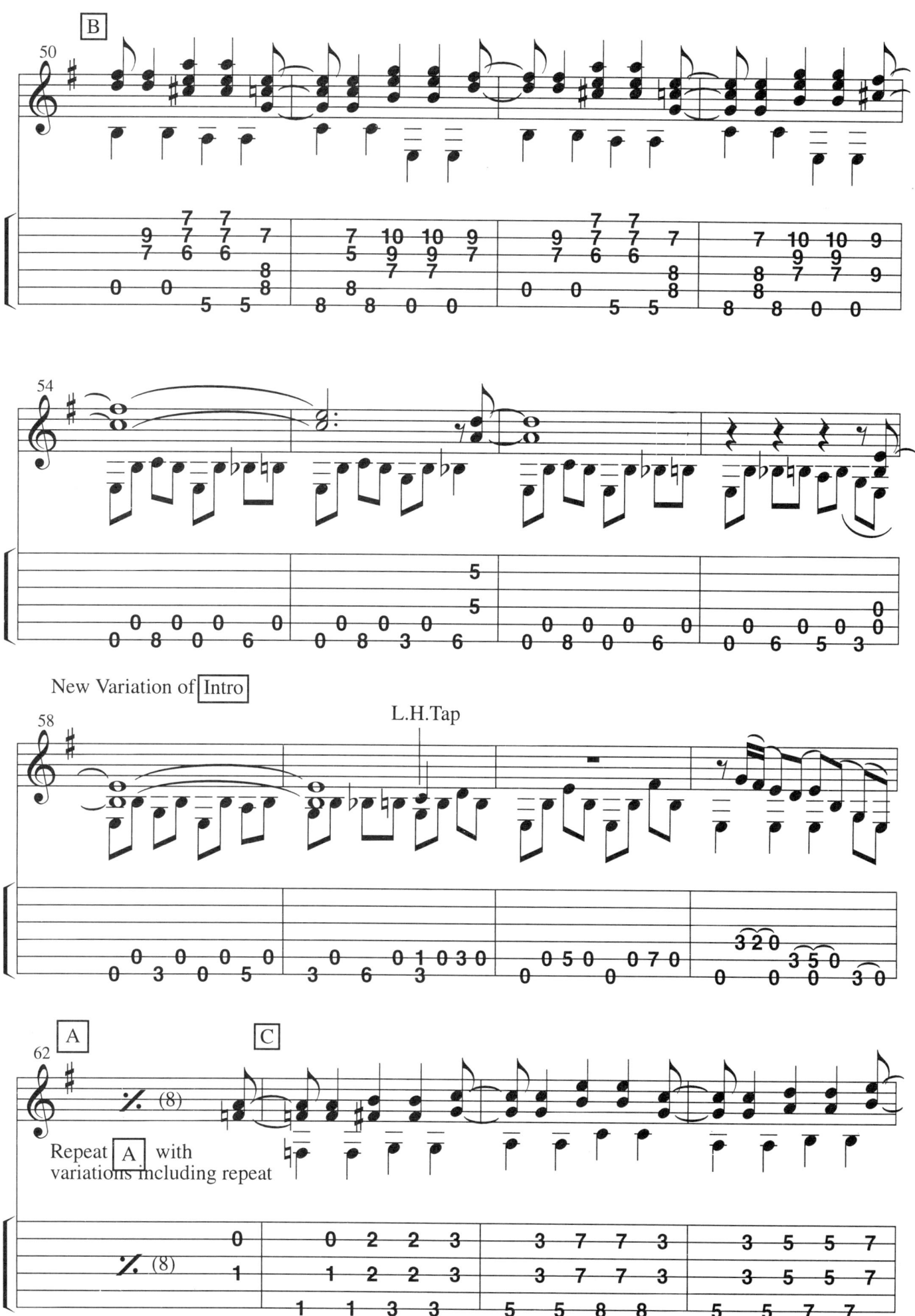

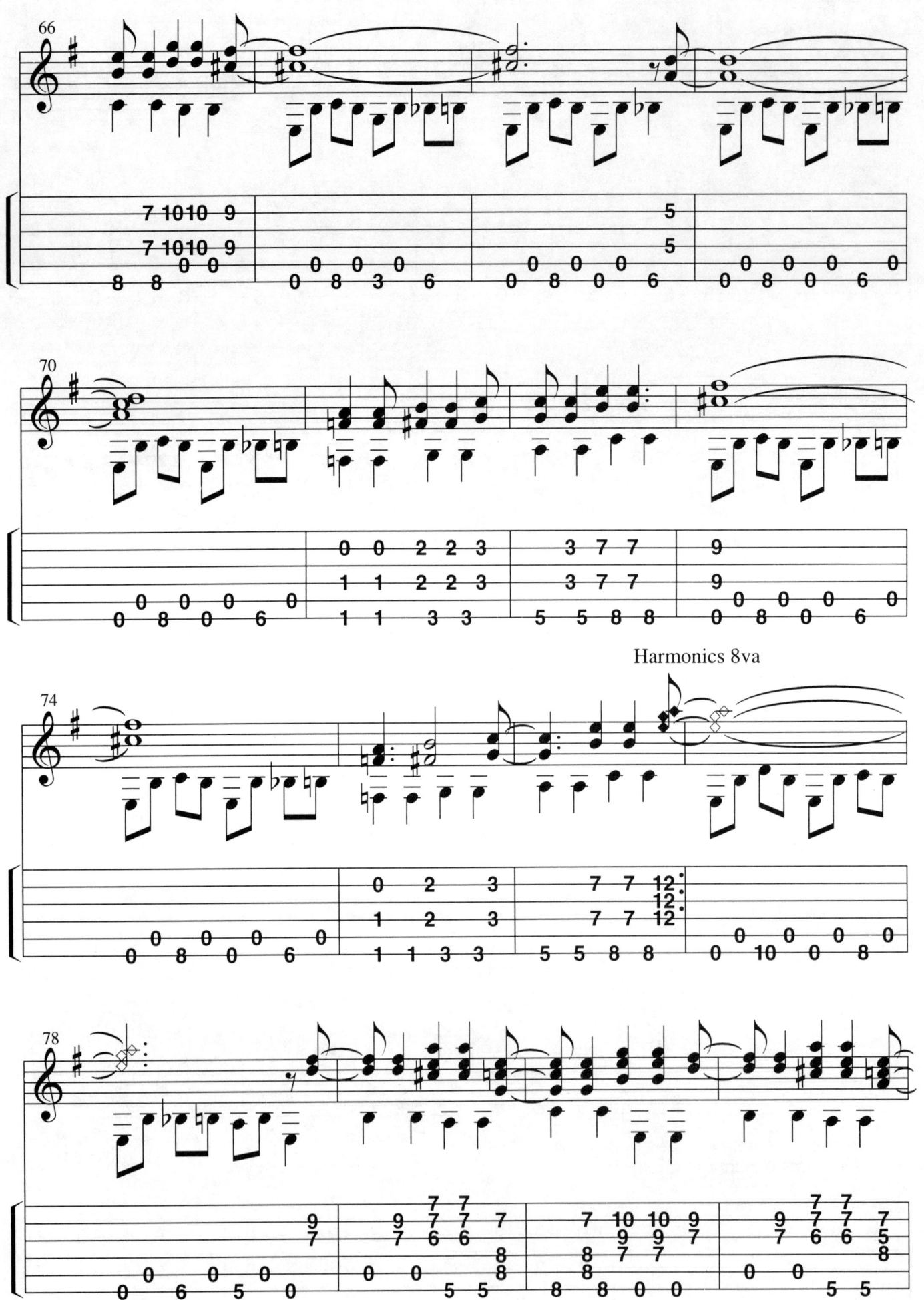

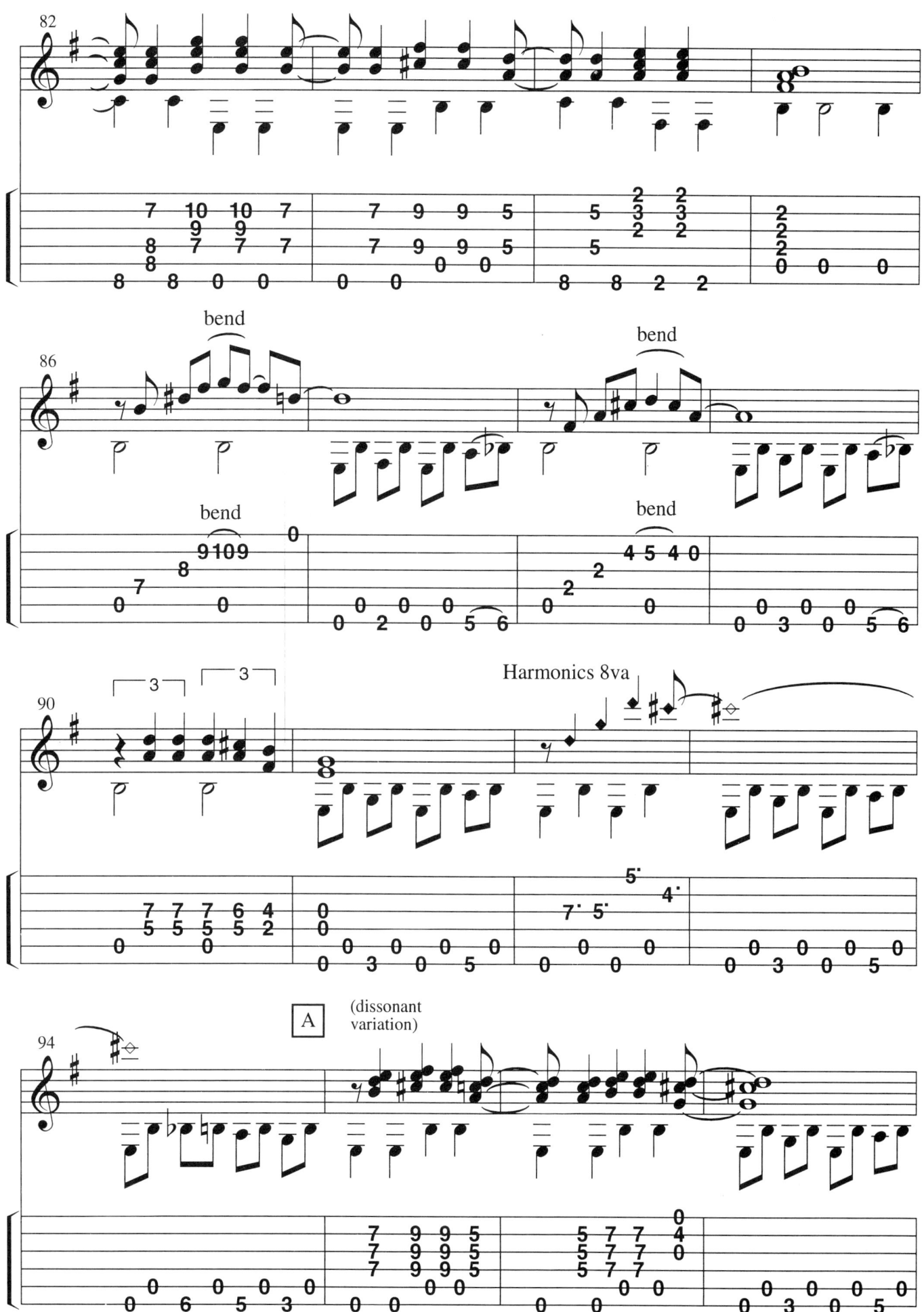

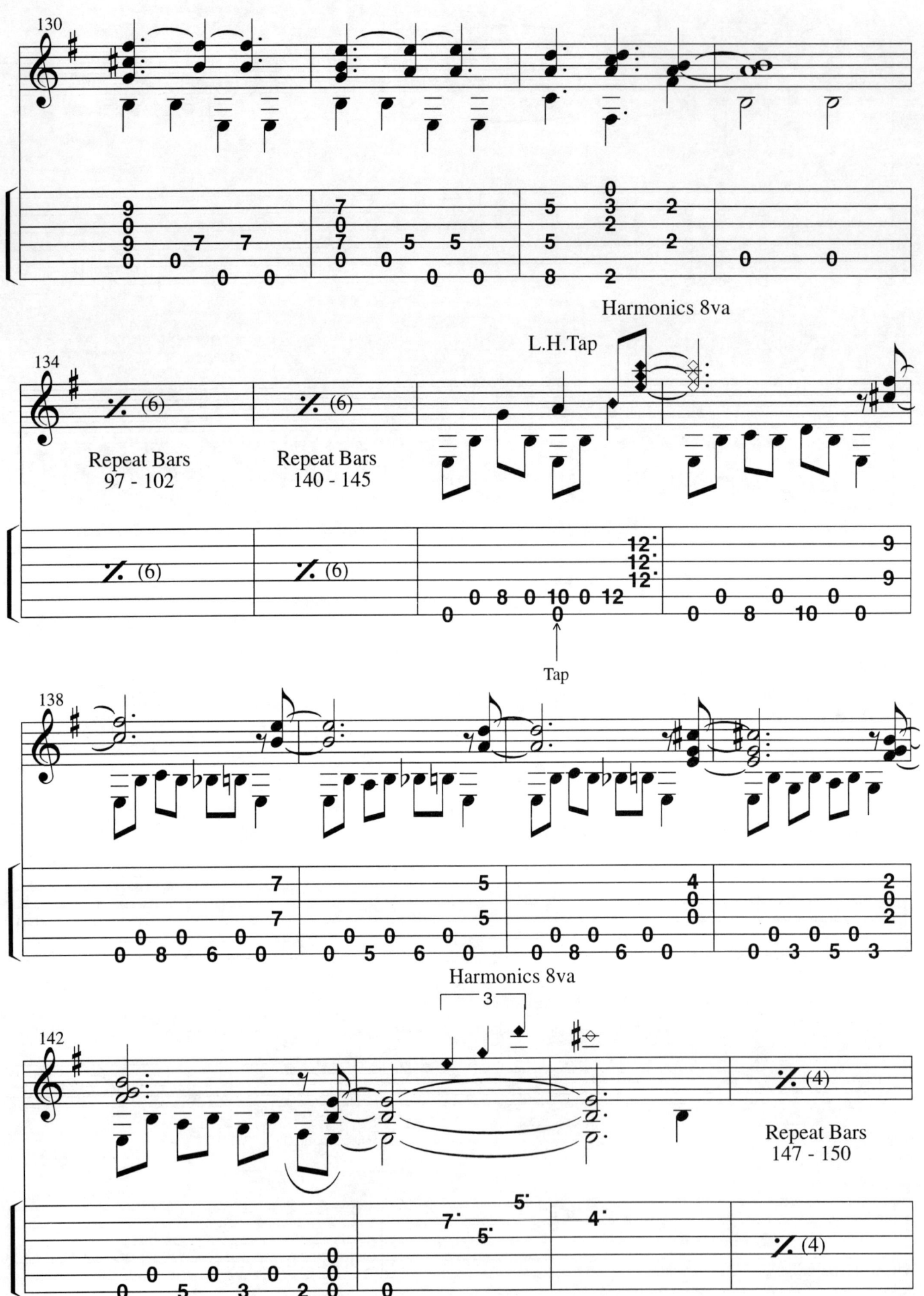

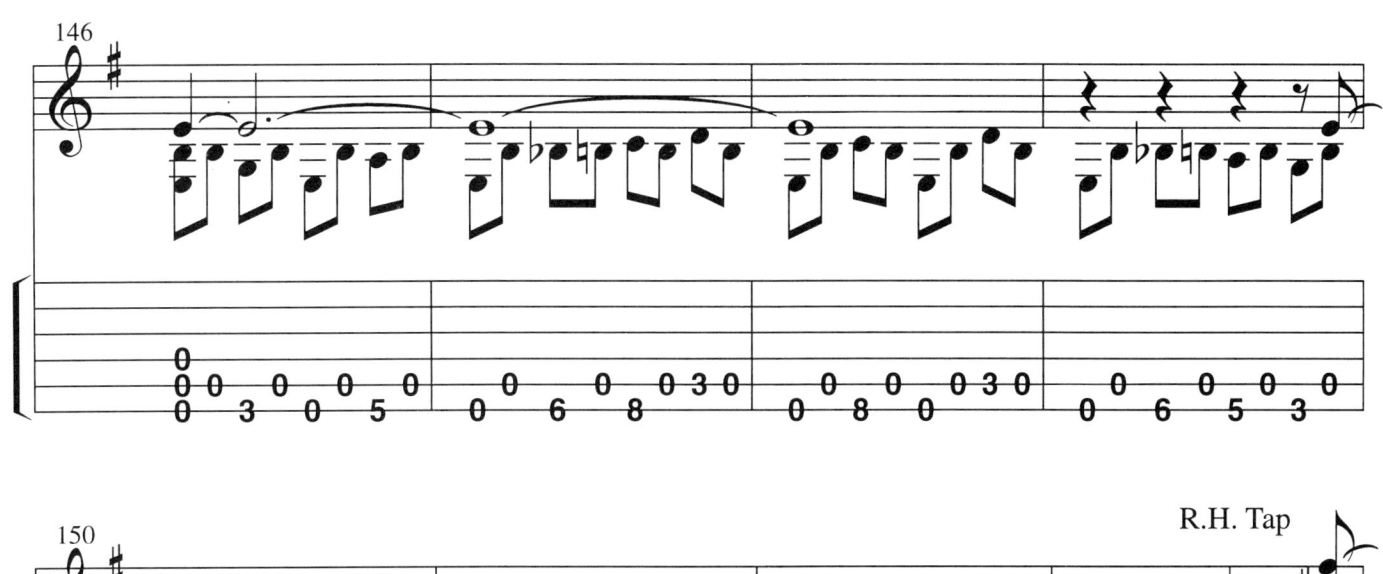

Repeat and Fade

* Chords are indicated for C and D, because player is expected to improvise melody every time C is replayed.

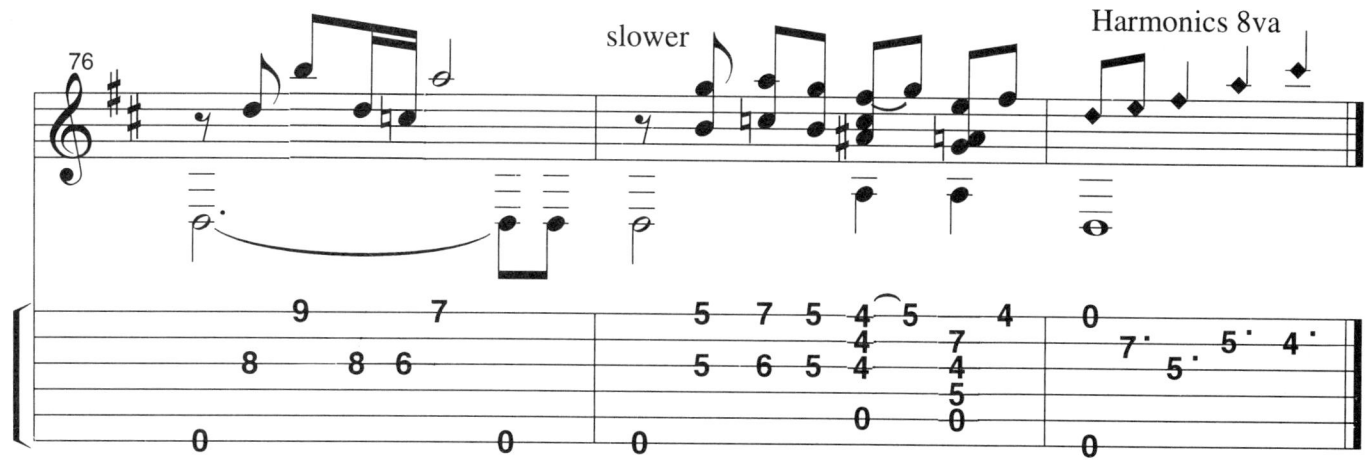

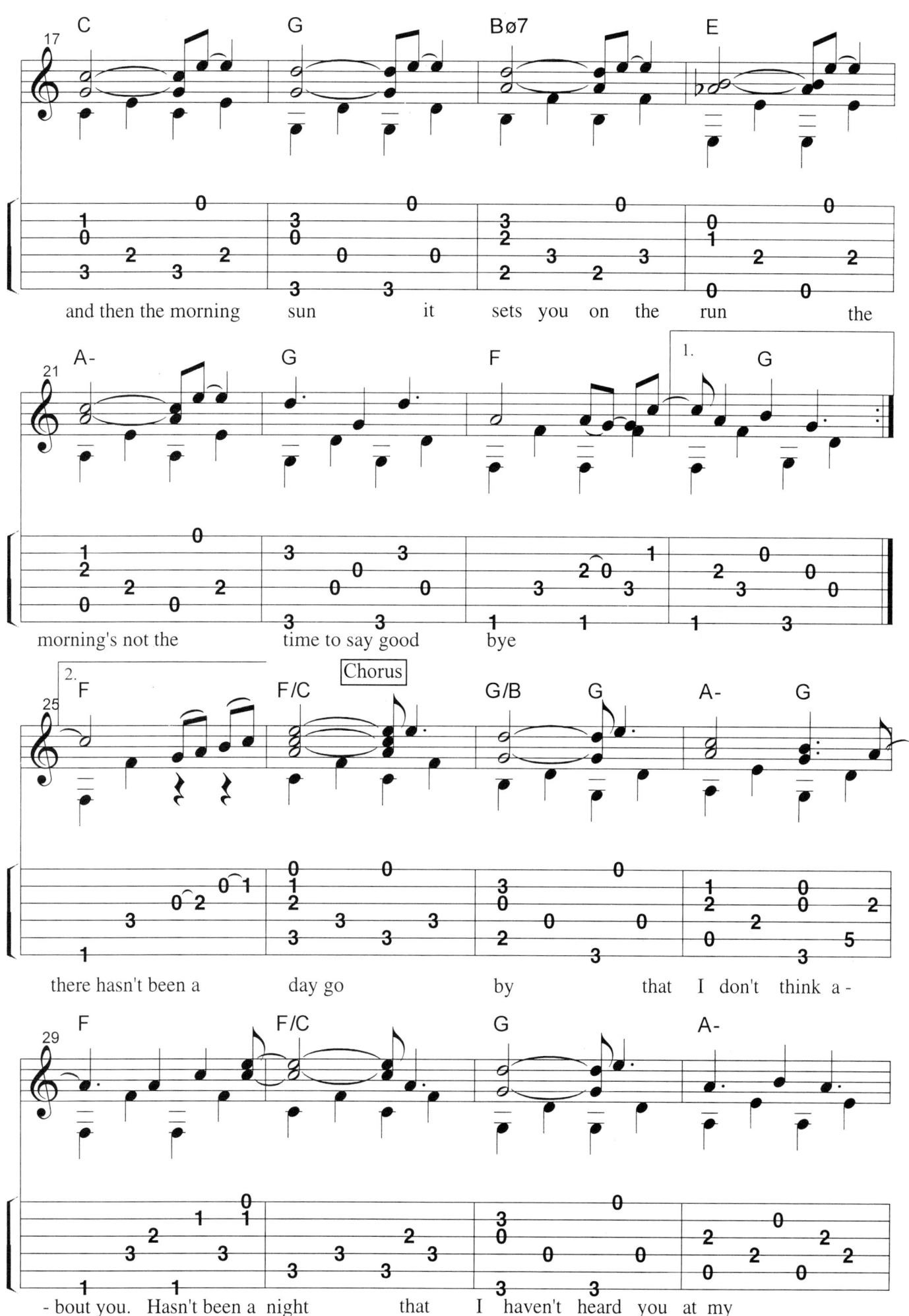

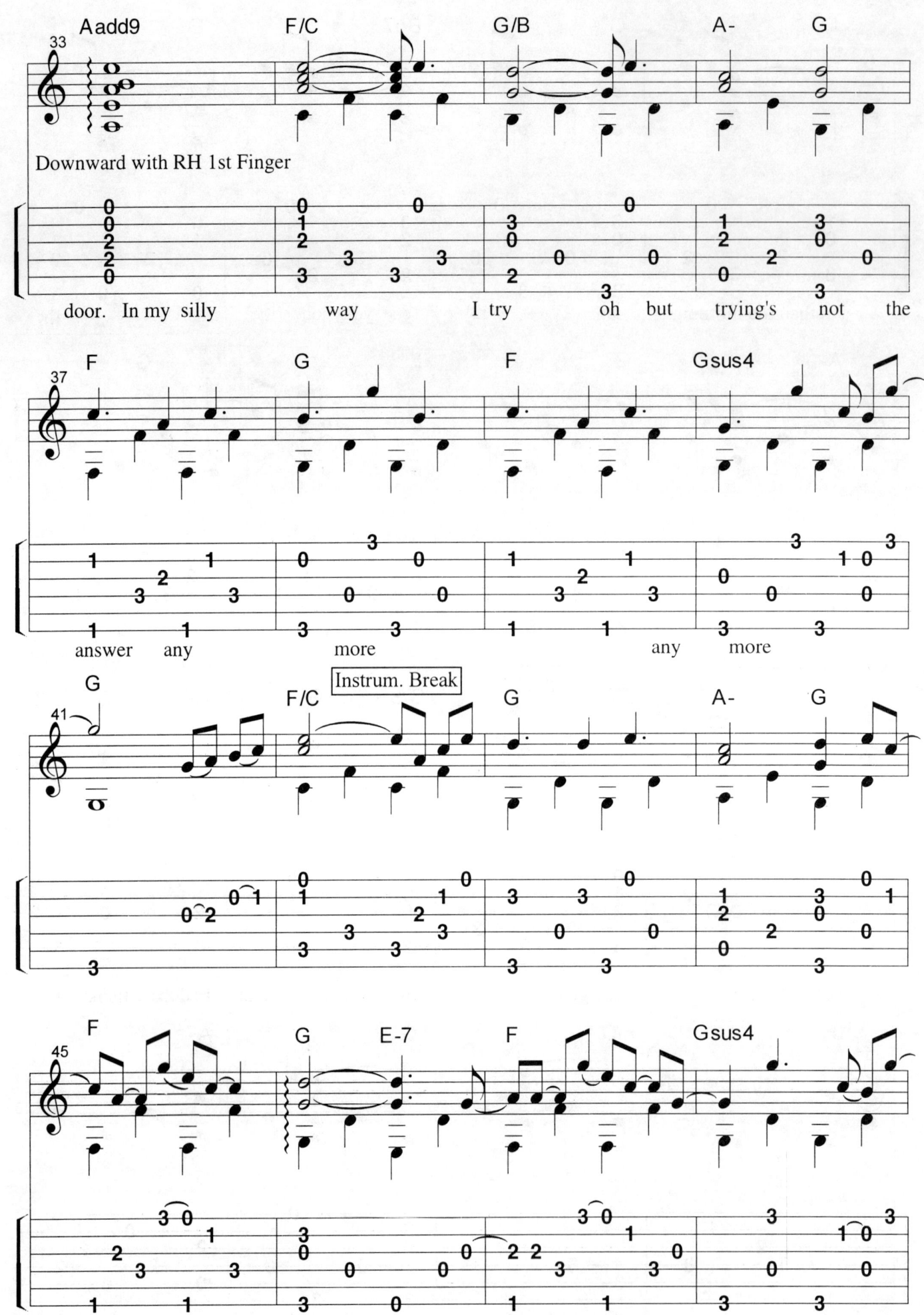

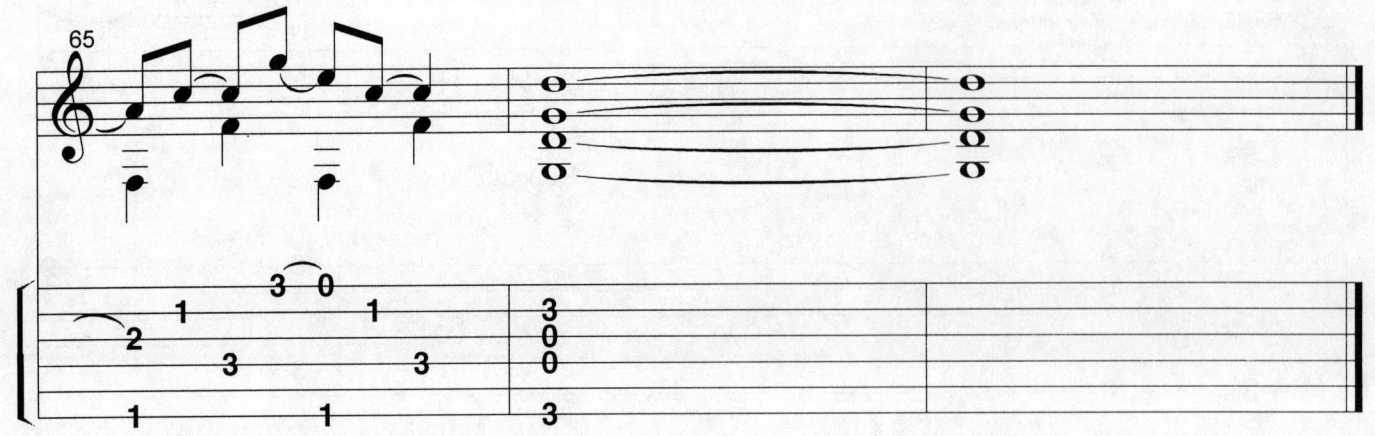

Anymore

Chris Proctor
VOCAL LINE ONLY

© 1997 Happy Valley Music & Sugarhouse Music. All Rights Reserved. Used by Permission.

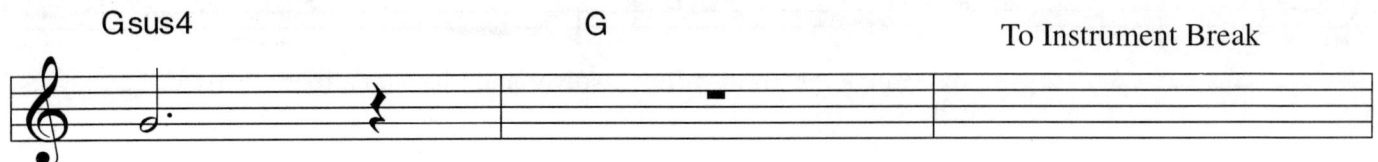

2nd Verse: A half a dozen colors paint a picture
And a half a dozen phrases tell a tale
But a half a dozen lies, how they turn you quickly wise
And they show so quickly where your wisdom fails.

Chorus

3rd Verse: The lovin' times are flowers in my garden
The petals chilled by an early fall
The winter winds they blow, girl they cover them with snow
It's a wonder when the springtime comes at all.

4th Verse: But now a hundred photographs have faded
A torn envelope, with a stranger's name
The debris of dreams inconsequential as it seems
Keeps those memories flowing onwards just the same.

Chorus